ON VACATION

by Genie Espinosa

WINDMILL BOOKS

Published in 2020 by Windmill Books, an
imprint of Rosen Publishing
29 East 21st Street, New York, NY 10010

Illustrations: Genie Espinosa
Text: Paul Virr
Editors: Samantha Hilton and Joe Harris

Cataloging-in-Publication Data

Names: Espinosa, Genie.
Title: On vacation / Genie Espinosa.
Description: New York : Windmill Books, 2020.
| Series: Lots to spot
Identifiers: ISBN 9781538391600 (pbk.)
| ISBN 9781538391624 (library bound)
| ISBN 9781538391617 (6 pack)
Subjects: LCSH: Picture puzzles–Juvenile literature.
| Vacations–Juvenile literature.
Classification: LCC GV1507.P47 E875 2020
| DDC 793.73–dc23

Manufactured in the United States of America

CPSIA Compliance Information: Batch #BS19WM:
For Further Information contact Rosen Publishing,
New York, New York at 1-800-237-9932

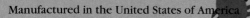

CONTENTS

Step inside a world of awesome puzzles!

For some, you need to spot the differences between two pictures. For others, you need to find the odd one out. You'll find all the answers at the back of the book. Turn the page to get started!

PLANE SPOTTING

Check in and find 10 differences before takeoff!

FUN IN THE SUN

Make a splash at the beach and
spot 10 differences.

WE ARE SAILING

Which of the super cruisers has
fewer passengers?

IN THE SWIM

Jimmy is ready to take the plunge! All of the outlines are a perfect match except one. Can you spot it?

ALL
ABOARD

Quick! Can you spot 10 differences before this train leaves the station?

BUILD IT

Which container has not been used
to build any of the sandcastles?

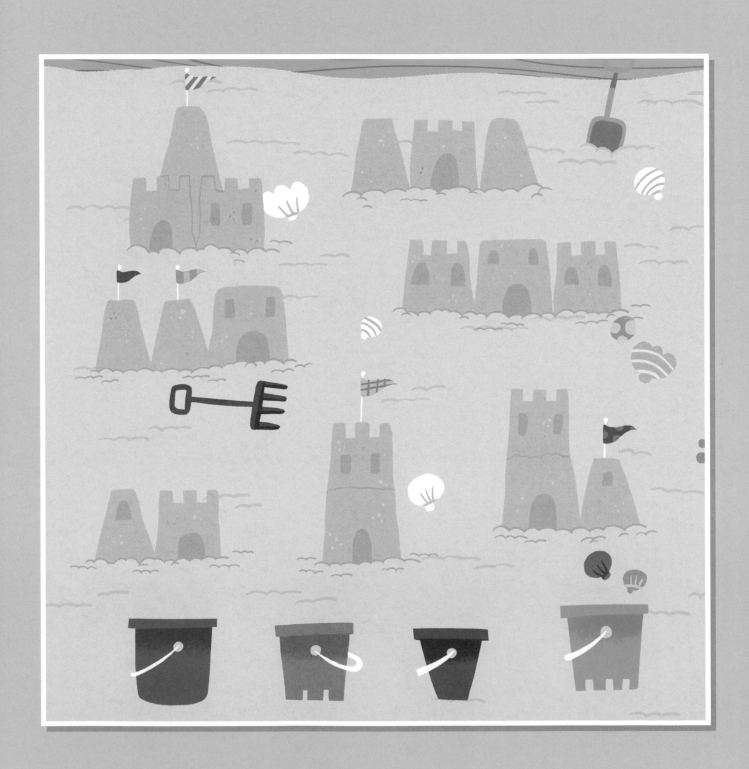

FAST FLEET

Can you find a single yacht that only has yellow, orange, and white stripes on its sail?

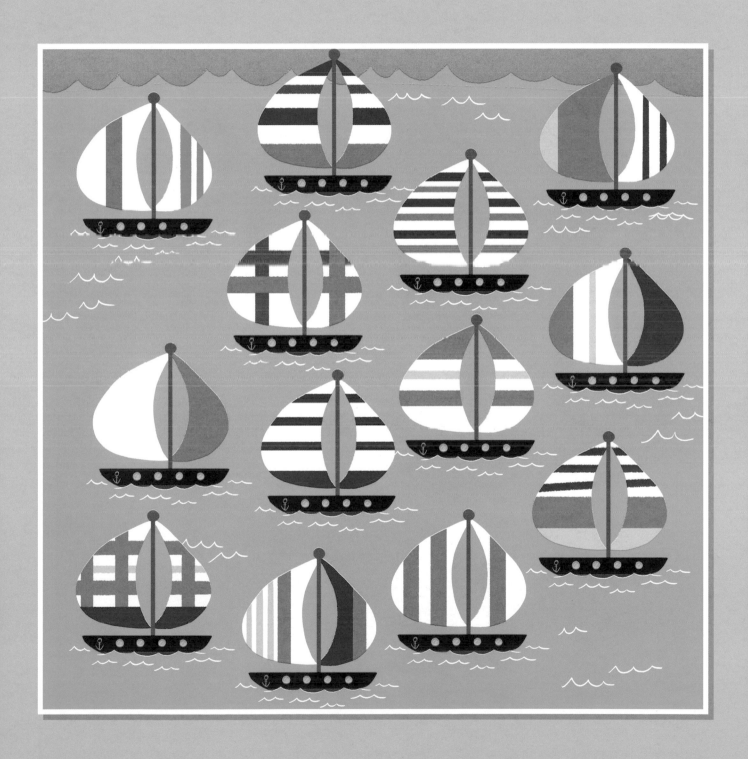

POOL PUZZLE

Splish, splash, and spot 10 differences
at the pool.

DESERT TOUR

Can you spot 10 differences across
the desert sands?

SNOW TIME

Check out Louis on the ski slopes!
Which of the outline shapes is not
an exact match for the main picture?

SUPER SURFERS

Which of the surfers' shorts do not match his or her board?

SUPER SPLASH!

Are you ready to make a big splash? Find 10 differences between these water park pictures.

EASY PISA

Which of the souvenirs has turned out slightly different from the rest?

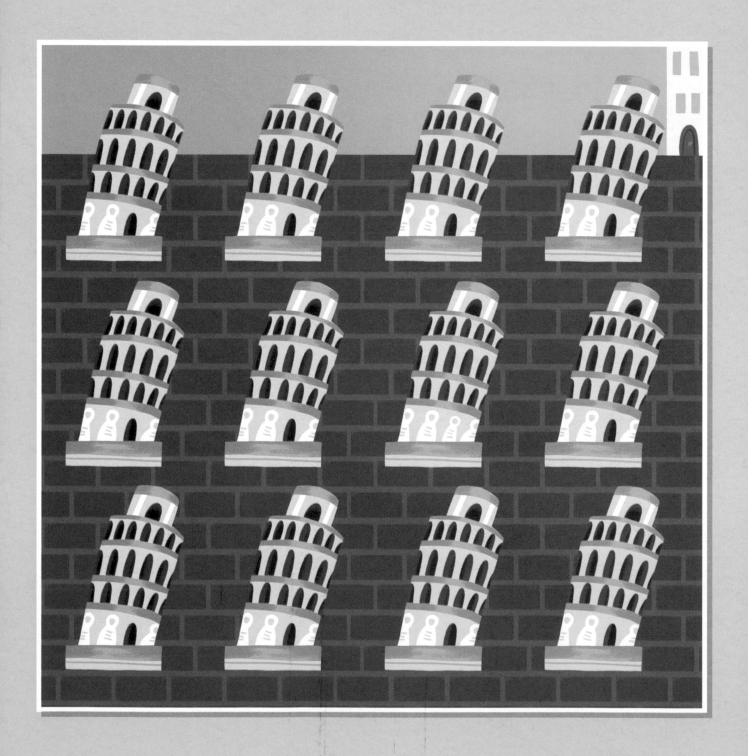

COLLECTION TIME

Which piece of luggage is missing its tag?

AMUSEMENT PARK

Hold on tight, this is going to be fun! Can you spot 10 differences between these busy scenes?

BALLOON SELLER

Pepe is looking for a balloon that looks funnier than the others. Can you find one?

FEELING CRABBY

Which of the comical crabs is a tiny bit different from all the others?

CHRISTMASTIME

It's time to decorate the Christmas tree!
Spot 10 differences between these festive scenes.

ALL AT SEA

One of the seahorse silhouettes does not match the main picture. Can you "sea" which one it is?

FINDING THE WAY

See if you're heading in the right direction to find the odd one out in this selection.

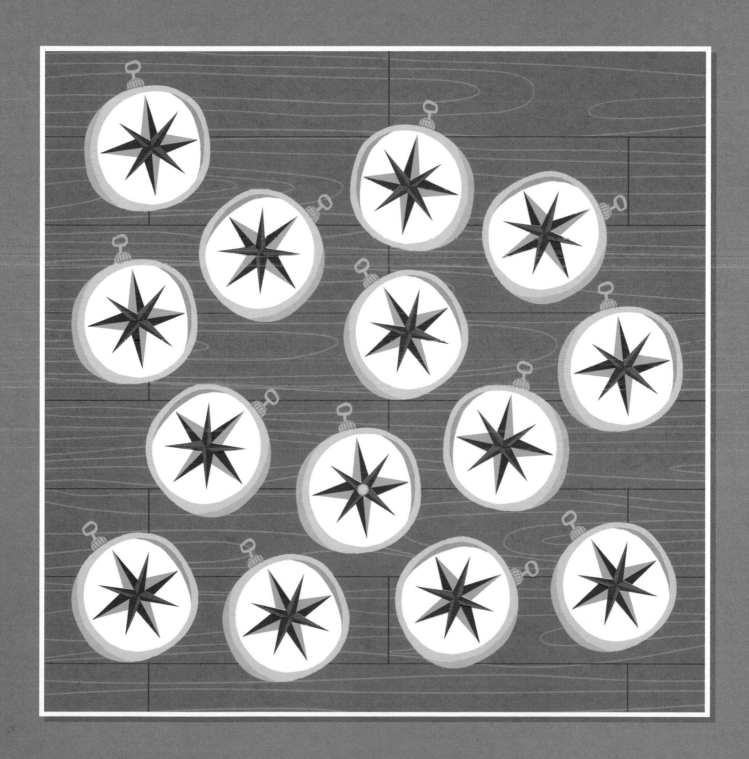

CORAL REEF

Dive into the sea and explore the coral reef.
Can you find 10 differences here below the waves?

ANSWERS

Page 4 Plane Spotting

Page 5 Fun in the Sun

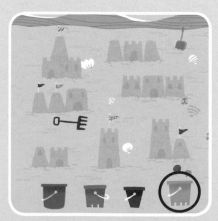

Page 6 We Are Sailing

Page 7 In the Swim

Page 8-9 All Aboard

Page 10 Build It

Page 11 Fast Fleet

Page 12 Pool Puzzle

Page 13 Desert Tour

Page 14 Snow Time

Page 15 Super Surfers

Page 16-17 Super Splash!

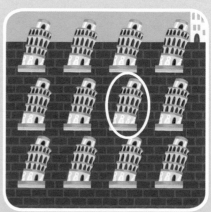

Page 18 Easy Pisa

Page 19 Collection Time

Page 20-21 Amusement Park

Page 22 Balloon Seller

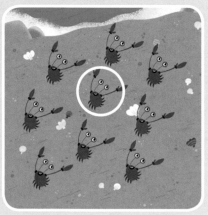

Page 23 Feeling Crabby

Page 24-25 Christmastime

Page 26 All at Sea

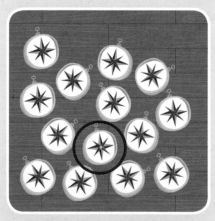

Page 27 Finding the Way

Page 28-29 Coral Reef

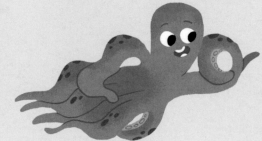